TUNDRA and COLD DESERTS

Rose Pipes

A ZOË BOOK

A ZOË BOOK

© 1998 Zoë Books Limited

Devised and produced by
Zoë Books Limited
15 Worthy Lane
Winchester
Hampshire SO23 7AB
England

First published in Great Britain in 1998 by
Zoë Books Limited
15 Worthy Lane
Winchester
Hampshire SO23 7AB

A record of the CIP data is available from the British Library.

ISBN 1 86173 021 7

Printed in Hong Kong by Midas Printing Ltd.
Editor: Kath Davies
Maps: Sterling Associates
Design & Production: Sterling Associates

Photographic acknowledgments

The publishers wish to acknowledge, with thanks, the following photographic sources:

The Hutchison Library / Brian Moser 5; / Nigel Sitwell 9; / Sarah Murray 16; / Nick Owen 26; Impact Photos / Geray Sweeney 6; / Xavier Desmier-Cedri 13; / Ken Graham 19; / Neil Morrison 23; / Christophe Bluntzer 27; NHPA / Stephen Krasemann - cover inset tr; / B. & C. Alexander - title page, 8, 20; / Dr. Eckart Pott 12; / Daniel Heuclin 15; / Eero Murtomaki 22, 25; Still Pictures / Francois Pierrel - cover background, 18; / Thierry Thomas 11; / C. Pal Hermansen 24; / Hjalte Tin 29; TRIP / N. Ray 17; / N. Price 21; / M. Barlow 28; Woodfall Wild Images / Steve Austin - cover inset bl, 7; / Nigel Hicks 14.

The publishers have made every effort to trace the copyright holders, but if they have inadvertently overlooked any, they will be pleased to make the necessary arrangement at the first opportunity.

Contents

The world's coldest places 4

Wildlife in cold lands 6

Living in cold lands 8

Antarctica 10

The Taklimakan Desert 14

The Canadian tundra 18

Lapland 22

Mountain tundra in Africa 26

Glossary 30

Index 32

The world's coldest places

The coldest lands in the world are the
Arctic **tundra lands** and the **polar cold
deserts**.

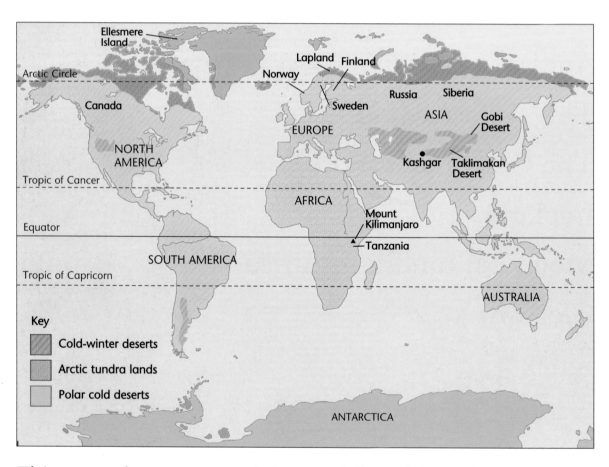

This map shows some of the world's coldest places. You
can read about some of them in this book. The names of
these places are on the map.

In the Arctic tundra, it is dark all the time in winter. The soil is frozen beneath ice and snow. In summer, the ice melts and lakes and pools form on the ground.

Most deserts are dry and hot all year, but some are very cold in winter. This picture shows the Gobi Desert in China. It is a **cold-winter desert**.

Wildlife in cold lands

No plants can grow in cold, icy **habitats**.
Plants do grow in tundra lands and on high

These plants are broad-leaved willow-herbs. They are
growing on Ellesmere Island in the Arctic tundra. They
flower in summer when the winter snow melts.

mountains. They grow close to the ground, out of the strong, cold winds.

The animals in cold lands are well **adapted** to living in snowy, icy places. Some animals have thick fur or feathers, and a layer of fat under their skin to keep them warm.

The mountain hare changes colour in winter. Its brown fur turns white. Other animals cannot see the hare easily against the snow.

Living in cold lands

Scientists and their families are the only people who live in Antarctica. Some people do live in the Arctic tundra and in cold-winter deserts.

This Chukchi family lives in the tundra lands of Siberia, in northern Russia.

Some tundra peoples still hunt or herd animals, but for most of them, life has changed. They now live and work in towns or villages. They can keep in touch with other parts of the world by telephone, radio and the **Internet**.

Some cold lands are rich in **minerals** such as oil and copper. There are mineral mines in the Arctic tundra.

Tourists visit some of the cold lands. They go to see the wildlife.
  This tourist is watching young gentoo penguins in Antarctica.

Antarctica

Antarctica is the coldest **continent** on earth and the largest cold desert. Ice covers almost all the land.

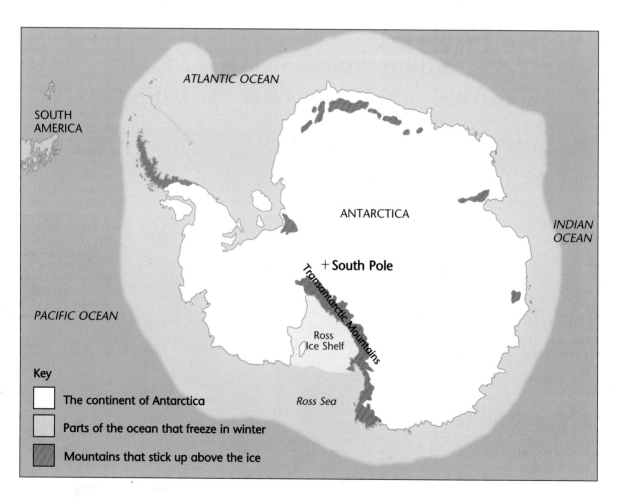

ATLANTIC OCEAN

SOUTH AMERICA

ANTARCTICA

INDIAN OCEAN

+ South Pole

Transantarctic Mountains

PACIFIC OCEAN

Ross Ice Shelf

Ross Sea

Key

The continent of Antarctica

Parts of the ocean that freeze in winter

Mountains that stick up above the ice

The ice is 3000 metres thick in some parts of Antarctica. Only the tops of the tallest mountains stick out above it.

There are no land animals on Antarctica, but seals and seabirds such as penguins have their young on the land. The penguin's thick feathers and fatty skin keep it warm. The female Emperor penguin lays its eggs in the autumn.

The male Emperor penguin keeps the eggs warm on its feet. It may stand in the dark and cold for up to 100 days before the eggs hatch.

Scientists in Antarctica live in bases, which are like small towns. There are schools, cinemas, and sports halls. It is so cold there that some bases are built under the ice.

Scientists from Argentina live on this base.

The scientists study the weather and the wildlife of Antarctica. In winter, many people leave the bases. They return in the summer, when it is light all day and night.

Ships bring more than 4000 tourists to Antarctica each year. They come to see the wildlife and the scenery.

This scientist is studying birdlife in Antarctica.

The Taklimakan Desert

The Taklimakan Desert is a cold-winter desert in China. Chinese people call it the

Fierce winds blow across the high, flat land. They whip up the sand into hills, called **sand dunes**.

Sea of Death because many people have died trying to cross it.

The desert is very dry. It is hot in summer, but bitterly cold in winter. Very few wild animals or plants live there.

Jerboas live in **burrows** in the Taklimakan Desert. Their sandy-coloured fur makes them hard to see against the sand. Jerboas search for food at night.

There is an ancient route called the Silk Road at the edge of the Taklimakan Desert. Towns grew up at **oases** along this route.

Kashgar is one of the oasis towns on the Silk Road. Markets are held here, like the one shown in this photograph.

Traders carried Chinese silk along this road. They used camels and donkeys to cross the desert.

Farmers grow wheat, maize, rice and other grain **crops** in parts of the desert where there is water.

The crops need shelter from the fierce winds that blow in the desert. This is why trees are planted round fields, and along the sides of roads.

The Canadian tundra

Canada's tundra is in the far north, close to the Arctic. Polar bears live on the coast.

Polar bears are good swimmers. They hunt fish and seals.

In the dark winters, the bears' strong sense of smell helps them to hunt.

The largest plant-eating animal in the Arctic is the caribou. Herds of caribou live on the tundra in summer, and move south in winter.

The Canadian tundra flowers in summer when the ice melts. The plants provide food for many tundra animals.

The Inuit people live in the Canadian tundra. They once lived by hunting animals and they travelled on sledges. Some Inuit still hunt, but now they travel in snowmobiles.

This Inuit man is on a hunting trip in his snowmobile. He is wearing warm clothes made out of caribou fur.

The Inuit people live in wooden houses in villages and towns. Food, clothes and light goods come in by aircraft. Ships and trucks bring heavy goods.

In winter, the trucks travel on roads made of hard ice. In summer, the ground is too boggy for the trucks.

These Inuit children are outside their school.

Lapland

Lapland is the name of the land where the Lapps, or Saami people, live. It is a cold land

Lapland lies in the far north of four countries, Norway, Sweden, Finland and Russia. This photograph was taken in Finnish Lapland.

with mountains, forests and lakes.

Many Saami people live in towns and work in mines or forests. Some people are reindeer farmers. They own herds of reindeer and sell them for their meat.

The reindeer move around, looking for **lichens** and other plants to eat.

The farmers leave their homes and move with the herds of reindeer. They set up camps to live in.

In parts of Lapland, the Saami meet together at certain times of year and hold markets or fairs.

The Saami people make clothes with colourful wool.
They wear these clothes for special occasions.

Tourists come to stay in the **holiday resorts** in Lapland. It is easy to get there by road, rail and air from the south.

People enjoy skiing or hiking in Lapland. There are trails through the woods, and cabins to live in.

Tourists visit the **National Parks** in Lapland. Brown bears like this one live in the Parks.

Mountain tundra in Africa

Even in hot countries in Africa, the tops of high mountains are always cold.

Mount Kilimanjaro is the highest mountain in Tanzania. It is 5595 metres high. Snow and ice cover its top all year.

The habitats change from the bottom to the top of the mountains. Grass grows at the bottom where the weather is hot and wet.

Further up the mountains, there are forests. Higher still, it is colder. **Alpine plants** grow here. There is ice at the very top of the mountains, so nothing grows here.

Some tall plants such as the giant groundsel grow among the alpine plants. You can see them in this photograph.

Some large animals, such as elephants, live in mountain forests. Small animals, such as the rock hyrax, live higher up.

The rock hyrax has thick fur to keep it warm. Black eagles and other **birds of prey** hunt these small animals.

Some of the African mountains, such as Mount Kilimanjaro, are in National Parks. Thousands of tourists visit these Parks every year to see the animals and birds. Tourists must be very careful because they can disturb and harm the wildlife.

There are villages and farms on the lower slopes of the high African mountains. It is too cold and rocky for people to live or to farm higher up the slopes.

Glossary

adapted: if a plant or an animal can find everything it needs to live in a place, we say it has adapted to that place. The animals can find food and shelter, and the plants have enough food in the soil and enough water. Some animals have changed their shape or their colour over a long time, so that they can catch food or hide easily. Some plants in dry areas can store water in their stems or roots.

alpine plants: plants that grow in cold places, usually on high mountains.

birds of prey: birds that hunt other animals for food.

burrows: tunnels underground, which some animals make to live in.

cold-winter desert: a dry place where it is very cold in winter, but hot in summer.

continent: one of the seven large landmasses in the world. They are Europe, Asia, North America, South America, Australia, Antarctica and Africa.

crops: plants that farmers grow to use or to sell.

habitats: the natural home of a plant or animal. Examples of habitats are deserts, forests and wetlands.

holiday resorts: villages or towns that people visit for holidays.

Internet: a network of computers linked across the world.

lichens: grey, green or yellow plants which spread across stones and trees.

minerals: things which we usually find in rocks, such as gold, copper or oil. Minerals are taken from the earth or rocks by mining or drilling.

National Parks: laws protect these lands and their wildlife from harm.

oases: desert places where there is water. The water may be in pools on the ground, or just below the ground.

polar cold deserts: dry places where it is very cold for all or part of the year. They are close to the North and South Poles.

sand dunes: hills of sand made by the wind. They are found in deserts, and next to the sea.

tundra lands: lands where snow and ice cover the ground all winter and only the surface of the soil melts in summer. The tops of high mountains are sometimes called tundra lands.

Index

Africa 26, 27, 28, 29
animals 7, 9, 11, 15, 17, 18,
    19, 23, 25, 28, 29
Antarctica 8, 9, 10, 11, 12, 13
Arctic 4, 5, 6, 8, 9, 18, 19

birds 11, 13, 28, 29

Canada 18, 19, 20, 21
China 5, 14, 15, 16, 17
cold deserts 4, 10
cold-winter deserts 5, 8, 14
crops 17

farmers 17, 23, 29
Finland 22
fish 18
food 15, 19, 21

Gobi Desert 5

habitats 6, 27
holiday resorts 25
houses 21
hunting 9, 18, 19, 20

ice 5, 10, 12, 19, 21, 26, 27
Inuit people 20, 21

Lapland 22, 23, 24, 25

Lapps 22

minerals 9
mines 9, 23
mountains 7, 10, 23, 26, 27, 28, 29
Mount Kilimanjaro 26, 29

National Parks 25, 29
Norway 22

plants 6, 7, 15, 19, 23, 27

roads 17, 21, 25
Russia 8, 22

Saami people 22, 23, 24
sand dunes 14
scientists 8, 12, 13
Siberia 8
Silk Road 16
snow 5, 6, 7, 26
Sweden 22

Taklimakan Desert 14, 15, 16, 17
Tanzania 26
tourists 9, 13, 25, 29
towns 9, 12, 21

wildlife 6, 9, 13, 29
winds 7, 14, 17